honey*bees*

Deborah Heiligman

illustrated by **Carla Golembe**

NATIONAL GEOGRAPHIC
WASHINGTON, D.C.

For my sister worker bees,
The Bucks County Authors of Books for Children:
Laurie Anderson, Liz Bennett, Pat Brisson,
Martha Hewson, Pamela Jane, Sally Keehn,
Susan Korman, Joyce McDonald, Wendy Pfeffer,
Kay Winters, and Elvira Woodruff.
~DH

To my honey, Joe.
~CG

When you see a bee on a warm summer day, do you think, "**Ow!** That bee is going to sting me"?

Don't worry. If that bee is a honeybee, she is after something sweeter than you. She wants nectar, the sweet syrup she finds in flowers. All you have to do is stay out of her way.

Have you ever heard the saying "busy as a bee"? That's about honeybees. There are many kinds of bees, but honeybees are the ones who work really hard—to make honey. In spring and summer, honeybees work about eight hours a day. Some work at night. Most of the bees in a honeybee colony are even called worker bees. And each worker has many jobs in her lifetime.

apple blossom

orange
blossom

dandelion

6

ORANGE
HONEY

WILD·
FLOWER
HONEY

This bee is a worker bee. Right now her job is to collect nectar and bring it back to her colony. The nectar will be made into honey.

But this is not her first job. She has had **many jobs,** and she is only **three weeks old**.

clover

apple blossom

Our bee's life began when the queen bee laid a pearly white egg the size of a pinhead. There is only one queen in every bee colony. She is the bee who lays eggs. Each day in spring and summer she lays about 1,500 eggs. She lays the eggs in little rooms called cells.

Most of these eggs become worker bees,
like our bee. They are all female. Other eggs become males,
or drones. A drone's only job is to mate with the
queen. He does no other work at all.

Our bee comes out
of her egg
as a larva.

She stays

in her

little

cell.

top-down view

Worker bees called nurse bees feed the larva royal jelly, which comes out of glands in a worker bee's head. Royal jelly is packed with vitamins and proteins. When the larva is three days old, the workers begin feeding her beebread, a mixture of honey and pollen from flowers.

side view

pupa week 1

pupa in cocoon

larva

egg

When the larva is about five days old, the worker bees cover the opening of her cell with wax. The larva covers herself with a cocoon. She is going into the pupa stage. During this stage, which lasts about three weeks, her body will **change and**

change and

change until she is a . . .

pupa week 2

pupa week 3

... grown-up bee!

The first thing she does is bite her way through the wax
and out of her cell. Then she cleans herself up.

Our young worker bee's first job is to clean. Bees don't like any kind of mess. And the queen bee will not lay eggs in a dirty cell. So young worker bees clean out leftover pieces of cocoon, wax, and dirt from the empty cells. Guess how they get rid of all that stuff. They eat it! Then they polish the cell. It takes from 15 to 30 worker bees about 40 minutes to clean and polish each cell. That's all our bee does for the first three days of her life—

clean, clean, clean!

Her next job is to feed the larvae, just as worker bees fed her.
Nurse bees not only feed the larvae, they also check up on them.
They check on each larva more than a thousand times a day.

(Are you OK? Are you OK? Are you OK?)

Beeswax is used in making:

crayons

fake
fruit

lipstick

crayons

fake fruit

Soon our bee's body starts making wax. Have you heard of beeswax? It comes out of glands in a bee's abdomen. Using the wax, she and her sisters build cells. In some of those cells the queen bee will lay eggs. In other cells the worker bees will store honey. **This is called the honeycomb.** The bees make sure the cells are tilted so the honey won't drip out. Now our bee is called a house bee. House bees fix broken parts of the hive and take care of the queen.

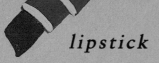 *lipstick*

crayons

 *fake fruit*

candles

The worker bees feed the queen, groom her, and even carry away her waste. When the hive gets too hot, lots of worker bees gather near the queen and flap their wings to cool her off.

fake fruit

crayons

Soon the worker bee doesn't make as much wax. Her main job now is to help unload the nectar older worker bees bring back to the hive. She will eat some of it and store the rest in honey cells.

To get the nectar, she has to beg for it from the older bees.

A beehive is completely dark, so bees communicate through touch. To beg for nectar, our worker bee drums her antennae on the antennae of a bee who has been out gathering nectar. At the same time she sticks her tongue into the bee's mouth.

The bee who has been gathering nectar has stored it in her honey stomach, which is separate from her other stomach. She now regurgitates, or throws up, the nectar into the beggar's mouth.

Bees use every part of their bodies to do their work—to take care of each other, to make honey, to communicate, to fly, and to guard the hive.

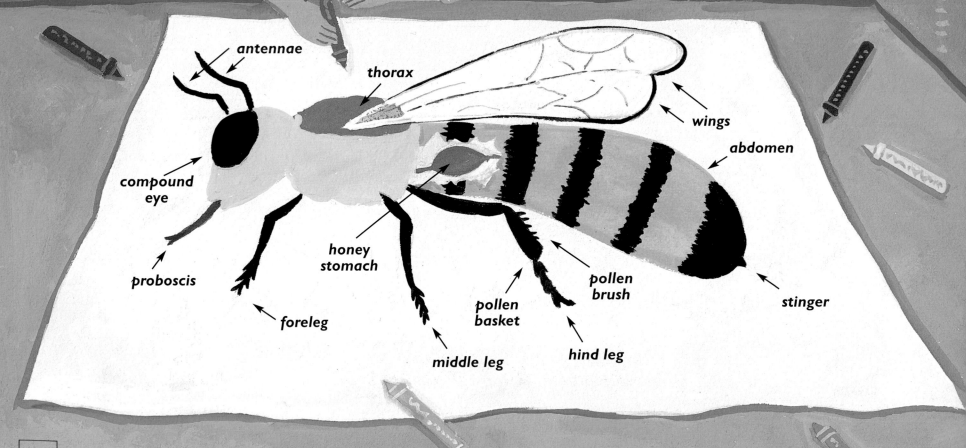

antennae

thorax

wings

abdomen

compound
eye

honey
stomach

proboscis

pollen
brush

pollen
basket

stinger

foreleg

middle leg

hind leg

robber bees!

robber bees!

When the worker bee is a little more than two weeks old, she becomes a guard bee. She places herself at the entrance of the hive with other guards. They raise their heads and forelegs. They look ready for anything. And they have to be! The guards' job is to protect the colony from wasps, ants, birds, and mammals, such as bears. But their worst enemies are honeybees from other hives who try to steal their honey. They are called robber bees. These thieves fly back and forth in front of the entrance looking for a chance to slip by the guards.

How can the guard bees tell these bees are not from their hive? They smell different. Bees in a colony pass the queen's smell and taste around when they pass food from bee to bee. So all the bees in one colony smell alike.

Sometimes guard bees need help fighting off intruders, especially big ones like bears. So the guards send out a signal through a special smell. Bees from all over the hive smell the signal and come to help.

Bees usually just chase away intruders. But sometimes they have to sting them. If a bee stings another insect, nothing bad happens to the bee. But if a bee stings a mammal, such as a bear or a dog or a person, her stinger will stay in the skin of the mammal. Part of her insides will stay there, too. The bee will die.

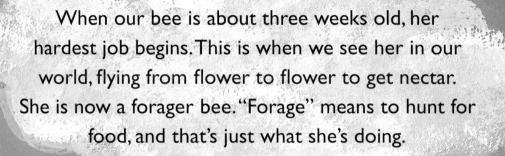

When our bee is about three weeks old, her hardest job begins. This is when we see her in our world, flying from flower to flower to get nectar. She is now a forager bee. "Forage" means to hunt for food, and that's just what she's doing.

The bee lands on a flower and sucks in nectar through her proboscis, a long, flexible tube on her head. She stores the nectar in her honey stomach. After she's collected as much as she can carry, she flies back to the hive. She shares the nectar with her sisters, who eat some and store the rest in honey cells.

proboscis

In the honey cells, the water in the stored nectar evaporates. The nectar becomes thick. That's the sweet, delicious honey we eat!

A worker bee usually lives for about six weeks in the spring and summer. She gathers nectar for three of those weeks, making about 400 trips altogether. In all those trips, she will collect only enough nectar to make about 7 grams of honey— the size of a packet of sugar.

Our bee also does another very important job while she collects nectar. When she lands on flowers, she gets flower pollen on her hind legs. Some of the pollen she scrapes into pollen baskets to bring back to the hive. The rest of the pollen rubs onto other flowers. Pollen from other flowers helps flowering plants make seeds and new plants.

Our forager bee is done for today. It's time to go back to the hive. She flies straight back—in a

→ **beeline.**

Look at all these bees. There are 60,000 bees in this bee colony. Most of them are worker bees doing their jobs.

The next time you see beautiful flowers,
or taste some delicious honey, thank a bee.
And the next time you see a honeybee
flying from flower to flower, remember,
she doesn't want to sting you.

She's too **busy!**

Dance Like a Honeybee

Honeybees communicate using smell, taste, and touch. Many scientists think they also communicate by doing special dances! When a forager bee finds nectar, she goes back to the hive to tell her sisters where the flowers are. If the flowers are toward the sun, she dances in a kind of figure 8 pattern. If the flowers are to the right of the sun, she runs up the honeycomb toward the right. The faster the bee dances, the closer the food is. Can you communicate with a friend without talking? Here's an experiment for you to try.

Here's what you'll need:

- "nectar" (something sweet, such as a candy bar, an apple, or a box of raisins)
- A friend
- A code (Use the code on the following page or make up your own.)

1. Hide the "nectar" from your friend.

2. Ask your friend to find the "nectar."

3. Help your friend find it—without talking! You can only move your body. Use a code to give clues. Your friend needs to know the code, too.

4. Now have your friend hide the "nectar" for you, and start over.

The Code:

Wiggle your right arm: *go right.*

Wiggle your left arm: *go left.*

Spin around: *go the other way.*

Move your knees up and down: *go upstairs.*

Point down: *go downstairs.*

Run in place very fast: *you're very close.*

Sit down: *you've just passed it.*

Squat down: *look under something.*

Use a mirror to read!

What Did You Discover?

Was it easy or hard to communicate without talking? Unlike bees, people use spoken language to communicate most of the time. But we also do communicate with "body language." We smile, frown, point our fingers. Can you think of other ways people communicate with each other?

To create her paintings, Carla Golembe used gouache on watercolor paper.

Text copyright © 2002 Deborah Heiligman
Illustrations copyright © 2002 Carla Golembe

Book design by LeSales Dunworth.
Text is set in Gill Sans. The title type is Bauer Bodoni.

Jump Into Science series consultant: Gary Brockman, Early Education Science Specialist
Honeybees expert consultant: Sue Hubbell, beekeeper and author

Reprinted in paperback and library binding, 2017
Paperback ISBN: 978-1-4263-2835-0
Reinforced library binding ISBN: 978-1-4263-2836-7

The Library of Congress cataloged the 2002 edition as follows:
Heiligman, Deborah.
Honeybees/by Deborah Heiligman; illustrated by Carla Golembe.
p. cm. — (Jump into science)
ISBN 0-7922-6678-1 (hardcover)
1. Honeybee—Juvenile literature. [1. Honeybee. 2. Bees.] I. Golembe, Carla, ill. II. Title. III. Series.
QL568.A6 H388 2002
595.79'9—dc21   2001001717

Since 1888, the National Geographic Society has funded more than 12,000 research, exploration, and preservation projects around the world. The Society receives funds from National Geographic Partners, LLC, funded in part by your purchase. A portion of the proceeds from this book supports this vital work. To learn more, visit www.natgeo.com/info.

NATIONAL GEOGRAPHIC and Yellow Border Design are trademarks of the National Geographic Society, used under license.

For more information, visit nationalgeographic.com, call 1-800-647-5463, or write to the following address:
National Geographic Partners, LLC
1145 17th Street N.W.
Washington, D.C. 20036-4688 U.S.A.

National Geographic supports K-12 educators with ELA Common Core Resources. Visit natgeoed.org/commoncore for more information.

Printed in China
17/RRDS/1

SAVE THE HONEYBEES!

Did you know that honeybees are responsible for more foods you eat than just honey? Without honeybees, many crops would have difficulty growing.

Sadly, due to many reasons such as the loss of honeybee habitats and climate change, honeybee colonies have been dying out. This puts many wild and agricultural flowering plants at risk.

WHAT CAN YOU DO TO HELP?

The good news is that there is already a lot being done to help the world's bee population! You can also help the honeybees by taking a few critical steps at home.

1. Plant many different kinds of local flowering plants in your garden! This gives the bees the best nectar for their environment, and a diverse mix of flower shapes, sizes, and colors is sure to bring in many bees.

2. Reduce your pesticide use! If you need to use pesticides, consider the type carefully and spray at night when the bees are less active.

3. Support beekeepers and buy honey! With recent bee decline, the operating costs of keeping bees have become very high, and beekeepers need your support, as well as the support of the local farmers who depend on their bees for crops.

DEBORAH HEILIGMAN is the author of more than 30 books for children and teens, including 10 in the Holidays Around the World series. *Celebrate Hanukkah, Celebrate Passover,* and *Celebrate Rosh Hashanah & Yom Kippur* were all Sydney Taylor notables. Her other award-winning books for National Geographic include *Babies: All You Need to Know* and *High Hopes: A Photobiography of John F. Kennedy.* She's also the author of *Charles and Emma: The Darwins' Leap of Faith,* a National Book Award Finalist, and *The Boy Who Loved Math: The Improbable Life of Paul Erdos,* winner of the Cook Prize for best STEM book, and an Orbis Pictus Honor. For more information, please visit deborahheiligman.com

CARLA GOLEMBE is the author-illustrator of a number of books for children. She has received illustration awards from the *New York Times, Parents' Choice,* and the American Folklore Society. She lives in Silver Spring, Maryland. Visit her website at carlagolembe.com

EDUCATIONAL EXTENSIONS

1. How do bees communicate with each other? Can you give an example of a situation in which bees need to communicate?

2. What is the role of the house bee? Why is it important to the hive?

3. The last, and hardest, job a bee takes on is as a "forager bee." What does it mean to "forage" in this case?